THE
BLESSED
MAN

A Collection of God's Wisdom

THE BLESSED MAN

A Collection of God's Wisdom

To God Be the Glory

Maxine

VINCENT BROWN
AND MAXINE BROWN

HUNTER ENTERTAINMENT NETWORK

Colorado Springs, Colorado

To order products, or for any other correspondence:

Hunter Entertainment Network
Colorado Springs, Colorado 80840
www.hunter-ent-net.com
Tel. (253) 906-2160 – Fax: (719) 528-6359
E-mail: contact@hunter-entertainment.com
Or reach us on Facebook at: Hunter Entertainment Network
"Offering God's Heart to a Dying World"

This book and all other Hunter Entertainment Network™ Hunter Heart Publishing™, and Hunter Heart Kids™ books are available at Christian bookstores and distributors worldwide.

Chief Editor: Deborah G. Hunter
Book cover design: Phil Coles Independent Design
Layout & logos: Exousia Marketing Group www.exousiamg.com

ISBN: 9798815976818
Printed in the United States of America.

Disclaimer

The writings of this book were compiled and disseminated by the author, Maxine Brown, in honor of her late husband, Vincent Brown. These were stories, messages, and teachings that he shared with her over the lifetime of their marriage. Author holds full copyright of written work. Publisher is not liable for any litigation in regard to this written work. All content is legally binding under copyright law.

Dedication

To my husband, Vincent,

According to Romans 8:28, God has a calling on our lives. God had purpose in mind when He made you. God conforms us to His purpose and to the image of His Son. You came into my life "on" purpose and "with" purpose. You lived a purposeful life—and you live on in my heart.

Your knowledge and love of God is evident throughout this book. You always believed that God does not look for ability, He looks for availability. I am honored to share your love of God with the world. I thank God for you.

Vince, when God made you, HE BROKE THE MOLD!

Loving you into eternity,
Maxine

Acknowledgments

"Trust in the Lord with all your heart And lean not on your own understanding; In all your ways acknowledge Him, and He shall direct your paths." Proverbs 3:5-6

Primarily, I give God all the glory! It is He who brought me through this journey to complete my husband's work. When I cried, He wiped my tears; when I fell, He picked me up; when I felt anxious, He calmed my spirit. God continues to give me the strength I need to navigate the waves.

To my wonderful family—Louise, Herman, Raymond, Gene, Ronald, Karen, Lanette, Hilton, Alvin, Barry, Phillip, Barbara, et al. Thank you for your love and support.

To my remarkable friends—Kisianga, Artina, Bettie, Gina, Greg, Reverend Annie, Dorothy, Charlotte, Gretchen, et al. Thank you for listening and for encouraging me to "just stand."

Foreword

"For God so loved the world that He gave His only begotten Son, that whoever believes in Him should not perish but have everlasting life." John 3:16

"Love suffers long and is kind; love does not envy; love does not parade itself, is not puffed up; does not behave rudely, does not seek its own, is not provoked, thinks no evil; does not rejoice in iniquity, but rejoices in the truth; bears all things, believes all things, hopes all things, endures all things. Love never fails. But whether there are prophecies, they will fail; whether there are tongues, they will cease; whether there is knowledge, it will vanish away." 1 Corinthians 13:4-8

I am so honored to bring this project to fruition. This book is about "love"—not a typical love story, BUT FOR the *Love of God.*

We celebrated Vincent's homegoing in March 2020. Pastor Robert J. Williams, Jr. spoke from the theme: "The Blessed Man." The message was poignant yet riveting. His life was a culmination of change for which we witnessed throughout the years. He wore his spiritual aura with dignity and respect. He did not flaunt, he persevered, and he blessed others along the way. Selfish? No. A giving spirit? Yes. God blessed him with a heart of gold and a sharp mind to discern differences with little to no difficulty.

Vincent and I always believed that your words must be ordained by God because life and death are in the power of the tongue. There are no bones in the tongue, but it has the power to break someone's heart. Being mindful of what you say negates the necessity to apologize. Summarily, ask God to ordain your words before you open your mouth to speak and ask Him to order your earthly steps. Then, sit back and enjoy the ride.

~Maxine Brown

Table of Contents

Chapter 1

Authenticity of God's Word

The authenticity of God's Word is confirmed by the Prophets who witnessed many historical events throughout the scriptures in the Old and the New Testaments of the Bible. In the first five books of the Old Testament, Satan tried to separate the people God created from fellowshipping with Him. Satan tempted Adam and Eve to sin. From the first act of disobedience, God promised a way to make things right again. God repeated this promise many times in the Old Testament.

The scriptures tell us of the many acts of disobedience of God's people and their continued disregard for the greatness of God and the beauty of His creation. God communicated with His people through the Prophets who advised them on how to live holy lives and warned them to obey God's laws or they would be punished. They continued to be disobedient and found themselves enslaved in a foreign land. Because of God's great love for His people, He freed them from slavery, brought them through a raging sea with dry feet, sent them food from the sky, and water from the rocks. God promised them a new King and an exciting future for their Nation. God repeated that promise many times through the prophets in the Old Testament.

The New Testament tells how God's promises were fulfilled. Eyewitnesses who saw God's promises unfold recorded exactly what happened. In the four Gospels (Matthew, Mark, Luke, and John), the writers report how God's promise of a new King came true. They tell about the birth of Jesus, and how He fulfilled the words of the prophets through His death and resurrection.

The most exciting part of the Bible is the last event, the resurrection. Jesus made it possible for us to fellowship with God by trusting Him as our Savior. It is also exciting to know, too, that Jesus now sits at the right hand of the Father as our Great High Priest and our intercessor. In the Book of Acts, the Apostles took every opportunity to teach about Jesus. Jesus told them to be witnesses of all that He had said and done. Then, He returned to Heaven and sent the Holy Spirit to give His followers the power to tell people about the good news of Jesus' death and resurrection.

Often, the believers reminded their listeners of the words of the prophets who told of Jesus' coming. One of Jesus' best-known witnesses was Paul—Paul was a man who tried to destroy Jesus' followers but became a true believer. Paul traveled all over the world telling people about Jesus Christ and starting new churches. Whenever Paul returned from a missionary journey, he often wrote letters to the churches and to certain individuals. These letters gave the churches the help they needed—gave more information about Jesus, and taught how to be good examples of the Christian faith.

The last Book of the Bible, Revelation, was written by John. John was exiled to the island of Patmos because of his witness for Christ. Christians need to know that there is hope for the future. God showed John many pictures from the future to give them that hope. The Bible begins with the Book of Genesis—showing us the beginning of the world. In Revelation, we see the end of the world as we know it. We see every promise fulfilled. Christ is triumphant, and Satan is defeated. The Bible truly demonstrates the authenticity of God's Word.

Chapter 2

Cleansing the Temple

The Temple in Jerusalem was a place for worship. It was a house of prayer for all Nations. Families traveled great distances to worship God, and to bring animal sacrifices for the High Priest to offer atonement for their sins. The Temple was also used to celebrate many of God's ordinances and traditional ceremonies. Jesus' parents took Him on His first visit to the Temple when He was only an infant. Under the law, each firstborn male child had to be dedicated to God one month after his birth. In the Spring of the year, the Passover was celebrated, followed by the Feast of the Unleavened Bread. According to God's law, every male was required to go to Jerusalem three times a year to celebrate these great festivals.

As Jesus matured into manhood, He visited the Temple yearly. The Temple had become a sacred place for Him. It was a symbol of His Father's presence. At the age of twelve, Mary and Joseph accompanied Jesus to Jerusalem for the Feast of the Passover. It was at this event that Jesus first realized that He was truly the Son of God. Year after year, Jesus came to Jerusalem for the Passover. On each visit, He had seen the Temple desecrated by the unscrupulous merchants who exploited the foreign worshippers. Finally, on one of Jesus' visits, He became so angry that He, with a scourge of cords in His hands, cleansed the Temple. He drove out the animals and the merchants who attended them. He then overturned the tables of the money changers. He said to them that sold doves, "TAKE THESE THINGS; HENCE, MAKE NOT MY FATHER'S HOUSE A HOUSE OF MERCHANDISE." Jesus was also angry at the dishonest, greedy practices of the moneychangers and merchants, and He particularly disliked their presence on the Temple grounds. They made a mockery of God's House of Worship.

It was necessary that the Temple be cleansed because it was being misused. God's House is a place of worship, NOT a place for making a profit. The merchants made a mockery of God's House of Worship and the merchant's trade overshadowed the main purpose of worship. Jesus took these evil acts in the Temple as an insult against God. The commercialism in God's house frustrated the people's attempt to worship God. Any practice that interferes with worshipping God must be stopped. These practices infuriated Jesus to the point of righteous indignation, and He took immediate steps to alleviate the problems. Matthew 21:12 records the second cleansing of the Temple which occurred at the end of Jesus' ministry. On this occasion, He said to them: "IT IS WRITTEN, MY HOUSE SHALL BE

CALLED THE HOUSE OF PRAYER; BUT YE HAVE MADE IT A DEN OF THIEVES."

Mark 11:11 relates the cleansing of the Temple to the cursing of the fig tree. The Temple was a place of worship, but true worship had disappeared. The fig tree showed promise of fruit but produced none. Jesus was showing His anger at religious life without substance. He compared the Nation of Israel to the fig tree. Fruitful in appearance only, Israel was spiritually barren. If you claim to have faith without putting it to work in your life, you are like a barren fig tree. We need to ask God to help us bear fruit for His Kingdom.

Chapter 3

Discipleship vs. Evangelism, The Cost of Following Jesus

Why do only a few people follow Christ for a lifetime? Why do some appear to follow Him for a while and then fall away? What prevents us from following Jesus wholeheartedly? Why do some of us prefer to build on the sand rather than on the rock?

It can't be that we don't know about Jesus. With all the technology available today, the archaeological research confirming the people and places of the Bible, the volumes of writings of believers explaining their faith, the exegetical study of the words of the Bible—it's as if we know so much, yet we believe so little.

Jesus wants complete loyalty, total commitment, and dedication. Some Christians seem to have one foot in Heaven and one foot in the world. They cannot let go of the things of the world. We must place Jesus at the top. Luke 9:57 gives some examples of the excuses given when Jesus invited select disciples to follow Him. The first thing Andrew did after he followed Jesus was to tell someone. We must come out of our comfort zone. We must not just sit in church, but we should reach out to the lost and to the needy. We must tell others about the Savior. It's a life of Evangelism and sacrifice of self.

You should understand that God sent His Son Jesus Christ to suffer and die for us. If you confess and forsake your sins and trust the Savior with our eternal salvation, you can pray and ask God to forgive you. You can read the Bible daily and obey what you read. Most importantly, you should get into a Bible-based Church with God-filled teaching and preaching.

Chapter 4

Divine Overflow

God created all things for His pleasure; He is worthy. The prophet Joel (Joel 2:15-24) delivers a strong message about the two sides of God—His judgment and His mercy. His message is one of warning, but it is also filled with hope. Joel wrote that our Creator, the omnipotent judge, is also merciful and He wants to bless those who trust Him. The people of Judah had become prosperous, complacent, and disobedient. Taking God for granted, they had turned to self-centeredness, idolatry, and sin. Joel warned them that their lifestyle would inevitably bring down God's judgment. Although the message was directed to the people of Judah, it is meant for people everywhere, even the Nations today.

September 11 had a devastating effect on this country. Whenever a Nation is in trouble with God, it always affects the economy. Judgement and mercy begin with the economy—the temporal things, then God deals with the spiritual. We should remember that God is the legitimate provider of all things—jobs, money, credit cards, etc. God sets you up materially to bless you spiritually. During a crisis, the answer comes from the prophet on how to recover from an economic slump, not from Dow Jones or Wall Street. Even your educated CEO can receive a pink slip. Your money is spiritual; your economic prosperity is contingent upon your relationship with the Lord. God wants to bless you and your descendants more abundantly. He is the sole source of our divine overflow.

We should always look to God for our help. We should not look to big business or to the Government's Social Security or Retirement Programs. Social Security is on its way out, so we need to be obedient to God. We need to pay our tithes and offerings. You should not go to Social Services. Go to the House of the Lord. In short, we need to repent. In 2 Chronicles 7:14, God makes it clear what a fallen Nation must do to regain His favor. It reads, "If my people, which are called by my name, shall humble themselves, and pray, and seek my face, and turn from their wicked ways, then will I hear from Heaven, and will forgive their sin, and will heal their land." True repentance is more than talk—it is changed behavior. Whether we sin individually, as a group, or as a Nation, following these steps will lead to forgiveness. God will answer our earnest prayer.

In Exodus 19:10, Moses was instructed to sanctify the people—Get them ready physically and to spiritually meet God. When we meet God for worship, we should set aside the cares and preoccupations of everyday life to dedicate ourselves to

Him. We need to participate in a National Day of Prayer and fasting. Corporate prayer will cause the economy of the country to turn around. Only then will God pour out His abundant blessings upon us. God loves the righteousness of His people. We have been called to be a "royal priesthood and a holy Nation"

(1 Peter 2:9), and we portray that royalty by honoring Our Lord, the King who gave it to us. This is truly our divine overflow.

Chapter 5

Effective Church Leadership

Effective leadership is recognizing that all people have different motivational gifts. Consequently, a good leader must also realize that his/her individual gifts cannot do the work of the church all alone. We, who are in leadership positions, must be willing to allow our strengths to balance the weakness of those whom we lead, and be willing to allow their strengths to make up for our deficiencies. As church leaders, we must be compassionate, faithful, and committed leaders if we want to develop faithful and committed workers. A good leader has a clear vision of what is to be accomplished and must provide opportunities for others to discover and use their motivational gifts to help accomplish the vision.

Effective leadership in the Church is inspiring and motivating people toward helping the Church grow. Leadership does not necessarily mean "taking charge or giving orders"—there are different ways to lead. You can set examples, influence others, provide encouragement, and introduce innovative ideas for problem solving. You can also help mediate differences and disagreements by encouraging a spirit of cooperation. Every Christian can and should contribute their time and talent to the Ministry of Helps. This would free the pastor and spiritual leaders to work toward realizing the God inspired visions for the church.

Effective leadership is influence. Every time you influence someone—good or bad, positively, or negatively—you are assuming leadership. If you are on the playground at school, meeting with a teen group at church, or in a ministry committee meeting, it is easy to identify the leader. Look for the person who is influencing everyone else. Often, that person is not the "official" or "elected" leader. Also, a title and position does not mean "leader." There are some corporate executives who are not necessarily leaders.

Effective leaders must have character, not necessarily charisma. Leaders come in all different shapes, personalities, and temperaments. Effective leaders have one thing in common—character. Image and reputation are what others think of you, but character is what you really are. Character is what you are in the dark. Character is the basis for credibility. Without credibility, you cannot lead anyone.

Leadership can only be learned from someone who is already a leader. Leaders reproduce other leaders. If you want to sharpen your leadership skills, study someone who is modeling what you want to become. Ushers beget ushers. Teachers beget teachers. Every Christian has a responsibility to reproduce him or herself. Leaders learn by listening. That is how they assess what needs to be done. Unfortunately, we do not always have alert ears because we have open mouths. It has been said that since God gave us two ears and only one mouth, He must intend for us to listen twice as much as we talk. All leaders are learners because they continue to listen. They continue to look for ways to improve what they are doing. When you stop listening, you are no longer a leader.

Chapter 6

God's Gift to His Church, God's Gift to Man

For many years, my knowledge of the work of the Holy Spirit was limited. I knew that the Holy Spirit was the third person of the Triune Godhead, but beyond that, I did not understand the purpose of the Holy Spirit in relationship to my life. I have since learned that when God saves us, He calls us into a personal relationship with the Holy Spirit. As new creations, God made us joint heirs with His Son, Jesus. We are His ambassadors commissioned to deliver the Gospel message throughout the world. In John 14:12-13, Jesus proclaimed: "He that believes in Me, and the works that I do he shall do also; and greater works (greater in number) than these shall he do because I go unto my Father – And whatever you ask in my name, that will I do, that my Father may be glorified in the Son." When Jesus was on Earth, He traveled only a short distance from His hometown. Consequently, He only reached a small number of people. However, when He commissioned believers to become His witnesses, the indwelling of the Holy Spirit made it possible to take His Gospel message worldwide. In Acts 1:8, Jesus said: "But ye shall be witnesses unto me both in Jerusalem, and in all Judea, and in Samaria and unto the uttermost parts of the earth." Believers must be Spirit-filled and be controlled and motivated by the Holy Spirit to effectively witness for the Lord.

The Resurrected Christ

The resurrection of Jesus marked the beginning of Christianity and the beginning of the New Testament. After Jesus ascended into Heaven, He made provisions for His followers and for His Church by sending the Holy Spirit to do all and to be all that believers would need to live victorious Christian lives. The Holy Spirit lives in us as our enabler and works in our hearts in such a way that our lives magnify the person of Jesus Christ. He is our power source—without His indwelling presence we can do nothing under our own power. The infilling of the Holy Spirit made a vast difference in the life of the disciples. Before the day of Pentecost, the disciples were a group of fearful, doubting individuals. Even though they knew that Jesus had risen from the dead, some still doubted. However, at Pentecost, they were filled with the Holy Spirit and the indwelling presence of the Holy Spirit caused them to be bold witnesses for the Lord. Likewise, it takes an indwelling presence for us to be in the Lord and to be witnesses who produce evidence.

In John 14:16, Jesus said "And I will pray to the Father, and He shall give you another comforter, that He may abide with you forever." In Chapter 16:7, He told His disciples it was to their advantage that He leave. When we review the works of the Holy Spirit in believers, we understand why it was to the advantage of His followers that He leave.

The works of the Holy Spirit named in the Scripture include: BAPTISM, by which the Holy Spirit unites us to Jesus; FILLING, by which the Holy Spirit strengthens us to live in harmony with God's will (Ephesians 18); SEALING, which presents the Spirit's permanent presence in our personality; and SPIRITUAL GIFTS, which represent the various ways that the Holy Spirit enables us to minister to others. In addition, the New Testament describes other activities of the Spirit in believers. He leads and guides us according to God's will; He is within us to transform us into Christ likeness; and His presence frees us and enables us to live righteous lives. Understanding the wonder of having God's Spirit as our constant Companion and Helper frees us to step out on faith, confident that we can make choices that will please God.

God Empowers His Church and Believers for Ministry. God gave the gift of the Holy Spirit to any believer in the Lord Jesus who has accepted Him according to Romans 10:9,10. The gift has already been given, now it is up to the saved to receive the gift. Salvation is the only prerequisite. God also made provisions for His Church by giving ministry gifts. In Ephesians 4:11, we learn that Christ gave some Apostles and some Prophets, and some Evangelists and some Pastors and Teachers known as the Five-Fold Ministries. These gifts were given for the work of the ministry, and for the edifying, exhorting, and maturing of the body of Christ.

In 1 Corinthians 12:27, 28, we learn there is a divine call to believers. God hath set some in the Church. Verse 27 reads as follows; "Now ye are the body of Christ and members. (28) And God hath set some in the church, first, Apostles, secondarily Prophets, thirdly teachers, after that miracle, then gifts of healing, helps, governments and diversities of tongues." Ephesians 4:11 says, "God Gave" – 1 Corinthians 12:28 says that "God Set." The Corinthian passage calls the Body of Christ the Church. The Church is the Body of Christ. The Body of Christ is the Church. God sets ministry gifts in the Church – not man.

There is a vast difference between God setting some in the Church and man setting some in the Church. Some churches are working to get back to New Testament practices and have established organizations which they call ministries. They call and set people who have no divine calling in these offices which sometimes causes confusion because it is unscriptural. Remember, God does the calling, and God does the setting. The ministry gifts are people—people who are called by God to the fulltime ministry. Those people whom God calls; He equips with spiritual gifts. These ministries are not based on natural gifts, but on spiritual or supernatural gifts. When a person is born again, God

22

has in mind what He called that person to do. With the new birth, one is given certain spiritual talents for him to stand wherever he is in the Body of Christ. Being filled with the Holy Spirit enhances that. God equips people with spiritual gifts necessary to stand in the office He calls them to. Jesus Christ is the Head of His Body, the Church. The Head and the Body are one; therefore, Jesus directs all operations of His Body from the right hand of the Father.

Living A Spirit-Filled Life

If we are to follow Christ, to have His mind in us, and to live out His life, we must seek to regard the fullness of the Spirit as a daily supply, a daily provision. In no other way can we live the life of obedience, of joy, of self-sacrifice, and of power for service. Christ came as God to make known the Father and the Spirit came as God to make known the Son in us. We need to understand that the Spirit, as God, claims absolute surrender and is willing to take possession of our whole being and enable us to fulfill all that Christ asks of us. It is the Spirit who can deliver us from all the power of the flesh, who can conquer the power of the world in us. It is the Spirit through whom Christ Jesus will manifest Himself to us in nothing less than His abiding presence.

Chapter 7

God's Love for Us

In 1 John 4:7-10, Jesus instructs us to love one another, for love is of God; and everyone who loves God is born of God and knows God. This is especially important because of the times in which we are living. The world is full of deceit, animosity, discord, and strife. It slaps us in the face every day. We see it in the White House, the Congress, our government, our schools, in our relationships, and even in our churches. Everyone believes love is important, but we oftentimes think of it as a feeling. In actuality, "love is action—not emotion." The most profound action came from God when He so loved us that He sent His only begotten Son to the world that we might live through Him.

God is expressing His love for us when He gives us eternal life. As John said, "God is love." God creates people to love. He loves everybody—He even loves sinners. God loves us so much that He made us joint heirs with His only begotten Son, Jesus. We can show our love for God by choosing to live our lives through Him. Jesus, our Lord, became an atoning sacrifice for our sins, so that we can live our lives with hope.

Jesus became an atoning sacrifice for our sins, so that we can live our lives with hope. Through the shed blood of Jesus, love found a way to reach the unreachable. Love found a way to cleanse us from sin that barred us from God's presence and fellowship. Love found a way to save us, to bring us peace, and finally to bring us home. Love found a way to grant us salvation, and to restore our right to fellowship with God. Love found a way when there was no way.

God lives through us. We cannot take His spiritual and material blessings for granted. If our cup is overflowing with God's love, we must pour that overabundance of love into the lives of others. As we continue to share God's love, He will continue to refill our cup with His spiritual and material blessings. God's Holy Spirit gives us the power to love; He lives in our hearts and makes us more like Jesus.

Chapter 8

Growing Up Spiritually, Significance of the Blood

In Leviticus 17: 11, it is the blood that makes atonement. The blood represents life itself. The New Testament speaks of the "blood of Christ" to remind us of Calvary, where Jesus gave His life as a substitute for our lives. His death paid for our sins. His blood cleanses us and makes us acceptable to God. The blood shed on Old Testament altars was a vivid reminder that sin must be punished by death. In the Book of Exodus, we learn that on the first Passover, a lamb was killed, and its blood was sprinkled on the doorways of Israelite homes. The blood in this instance was so significant that the angel who struck the firstborn sons of Egypt saw the blood and "passed over" those homes. The blood was also a promise that one day, God would take that punishment for us.

Old Testament

In the Old Testament, God instructed Moses to construct a Tabernacle where the Israelites could worship and offer sacrifices to God. In Matthew 25:51, the Tabernacle is described as having three parts—the courts, the Holy Place (where the priests carried their duties), and the Holy of Holies (the innermost room) where only the high priest could enter. The high priest could enter the innermost room one day each year to atone for the Nation's sins. The only access to God was through the high priest who offered a sacrifice consisting of the blood of lambs and goats to atone for his own sins and for the sins of his people. This ritual, according to Hebrews 9:9, states that it was symbolic for the present time in which both gifts and sacrifices are offered which cannot make him who performed the service perfect regarding the conscience. The people had to keep dietary laws and ceremonial cleansing laws until Christ came with God's new and better way.

New Testament

With the coming of Jesus Christ, God entered a new covenant with all believers including the Gentiles. Christ removed sin that barred us from God's presence and fellowship. But we must accept His sacrifice for us. By believing in Him, we are no longer guilty but cleansed and made whole. His sacrifice makes the way for us to have eternal life. Jesus guarantees our access to God the Father. He intercedes for us so we can boldly come to the Father with needs and desires. God responds to us through Heaven's best. He gives us His walking word, His printed work,

His indwelling word, the five-fold ministries, and 72,000 angels to watch over us. Most of all, through the shed blood of Jesus, our sins are purged, never to be remembered.

Chapter 9

God's Plan for Salvation- Heaven is a Prepared Place for a Prepared People

The theme of this writing is "Heaven is a Prepared Place for a Prepared People." It includes: (1) A Plan of Salvation; (2) An explanation of the difference between Praise and Worship; and (3) An emphasis on the Value of Entering into the Holy of Holies.

Introduction

On the sixth day of Creation, God made the heavens and the earth ready for habitation. In Genesis 1:26, God said, "Let us make man in our image, according to our likeness; let them have dominion over the fish of the sea, over the birds of the air, over the cattle, and over all the earth and over every creeping thing that creeps on the earth."

A Prepared Place for a Prepared People

In Genesis 2:8, the Lord God planted a garden eastward in Eden, where He put the man He had created. The Garden of Eden was a miniature heaven in which a bond of fellowship was established between God and man. The Garden of Eden was a showcase of the magnificent beauty that God intended for His Creation. Initially, man knew of no sin, sickness, poverty, fear, schism, or any kind of worry.

God loved man, and He prepared The Garden of Eden for man to fellowship with Him. Since man was created in the likeness of God, he was without sin. Because of Adam's innocence, he was able to fully enjoy all the fruits of the garden if he remained obedient to God. God gave him dominion over the garden and all that He had created therein. The only condition God placed on Adam was that he not eat from the tree of the knowledge of good and evil. But we all know that did not happen. Adam disobeyed God. Therefore, Adam and Eve learned by painful experience that because God is holy and hates sin, He must punish sinners. The rest of the book of Genesis recounts painful stories of lives destroyed because of sin. Disobedience breaks our fellowship with God. Fortunately, when we disobey, God is willing to forgive us and restore our relationship with Him.

God removed the sin barrier, and prepared mankind to enter Heaven through His Son, Jesus Christ. Through the shed blood of Jesus, man was restored in his original state. We can verify this truth in Romans 5:8, which says: "But God demonstrated His love for us, while we were still sinners, Christ died for us. The Bible tells us that the penalty of sin and its power over us was destroyed by Christ on the Cross. Through faith in Christ, we stand acquitted, "not guilty" before God (Romans 3:21,22). Because of Christ's resurrection, our bodies will also be raised from the dead (1Corinthians 15:2-23) and that we have been given the power to live as Christians now. Our eternal life with Christ is certain because God has given us a "Plan of Salvation."

Plan of Salvation

Salvation (Romans 10:9,10) is a term that means much more than forgiveness of sin. It was God's plan to restore man back to His original condition before the fall of Adam. Man was spiritually alive before Adam sinned. After the sin of Adam, man was completely cut off from God, but God had a *Plan of Salvation* in mind. Before the formation of the world, it was foreordained that the only begotten Son of God, Jesus, would be the Savior of all mankind. Jesus, through His death, burial, and resurrection, would be a living sacrifice for the redemption of mankind. Until then, man was spiritually dead.

There are some conditions man must meet to be saved. We must first repent by turning away from sin and having faith in the shed blood of Jesus Christ to wash away our sins. We are then justified as if we had never sinned. Secondly, we must believe that God raised Jesus from the dead, and then, we must accept Jesus as our Lord and ruler over our lives. The Bible says in John

1:12, "But as many as receive Him, to them He gave the power to become the sons of God, even to them that believe on His Name." All who welcome Jesus Christ as Lord of their lives are reborn spiritually, receiving new life from God. Through faith in Christ, this new birth changes us from the inside out—rearranging our attitudes, desires, and our motives. Being born again makes you spiritually alive.

The Bible tells us in Romans 10:9,10, "That if thou shalt confess with our mouth the Lord Jesus and believe in thine heart that God hath raised Him (Jesus) from the dead, thou shalt be saved." "For with the heart man believeth unto righteousness and with the mouth confession is made unto salvation." The Bible tells us in 2 Corinthians 5:17 that "therefore, if any man be in Christ, he is a new creature. Old things are passed away, behold all things are become new." Upon this act of faith, we are adopted into the family of God, we are in the Body of Christ, and we become children of God. God's *Plan of Salvation* contains anything we need from God to restore us to right-standing with God. The benefits of salvation touch every conceivable area of our lives. The more we find out about the subject of salvation, the more we realize the goodness, mercy, and ultimate wisdom of our loving Heavenly Father.

Praise and Worship

Praise and worship are important to God. Praise relates to God's character, who He is, what He has already done for us, and what He can do for us. The Bible says that the names used in

Old Testament times were to summarize the character manifested in the lives of believers. God's many names reflect His character to help us fully thank Him through praise and worship. Each of God's compound names represents reasons to give Him thanks. Jesus came to manifest the Holy Names of God to every one of us. We need to praise the Lord for His many spiritual and material blessings. It is also important that we know that we gain eternal life from God our Father through His Son, Jesus Christ.

Praise and worship prepare our hearts for the reception of the *Rhema* by preparing the human spirit to hear what God is trying to communicate to us. If we have problems, we should praise God and prepare a way for Him to intervene just as Paul and Silas did. We must invite God into our presence. The presence of God is paramount in our church services. Any church service without praise is pointless because God is not present. God is a Holy God; He cannot inhabit an unholy atmosphere which is tainted and corrupted with impure speech and thoughts. The protocol for meeting God is to come into His presence with praise and singing.

In Ephesians 6, Christ delegated the authority on Earth to the Church. By the very principles of delegation, God does not move or operate without the Church. A church must be victorious. Jesus said in Luke 10;19, "Behold, I give unto you power to tread on serpents and scorpions and over all the power of the enemy. Nothing by any means shall hurt you." It is the churches' responsibility to use its authority to tear down the strongholds of Satan.

Worship in the verb form means to pay homage, respect, adore, magnify, and exalt. It states in Terry Law's book that the Power of Praise and Worship is impossible to understand without relating it to an attitude of the body. Sometimes, it refers to a stretching out of the hands toward God. Sometimes, it refers to a bending knee. In Leviticus 9:24, the people fell face down before the power of the Lord. God made man to worship. He is essentially a worshiping creature. It is a part of his nature. His choice is not whether he will worship, but only whom he will worship. God demands our worship. He will not share our worship with anyone or anything.

When the devil tried to tempt Jesus in the wilderness and said, "All these kingdoms of the world will I give you if you bow down and worship me." Jesus responded to him, "Get thee hence, Satan: for it is written, thou shall worship the Lord thy God, and Him only shalt thou serve," (Matthew 4:10). This illustrates the principle of worship. Whatever we worship we ultimately end up serving. We cannot change our nature. Our nature demands that we worship something. Our choice is whether we worship God or Satan. Down through the ages, man has worshiped many things other than God. He has worshiped idols; he has worshiped his physical desires; he has worshiped money and possessions, political leaders, and false religion. In short, if we worship anyone or anything other than God, we are worshiping the devil because all false worship is dictated and controlled by Satan.

In Revelation 7:9-12, John saw a multitude from the great tribulation standing before the throne. They were clothed in white robes, with palm branches in their hands and crying with a loud voice, saying, "Salvation belongs to our God who sits on the throne and to the Lamb." In Verse 11, all the angels stood around the throne and the elders and the four living creatures, and they fell on their faces before the throne worshiping and giving thanksgiving and honor to God.

It is difficult to describe what worship really is. It is easier, however, to describe how we worship. We can bow down to worship. We can kneel to worship. We can lie prostrate or supine to worship. But even as we focus on the position, i.e., bowing, kneeling, or lying down, that is not what worshiping is all about. When we worship, we are simply responding to God. We are fine tuning our relationship with God. Our relationship with God is an intimate one and cannot be duplicated from one to the other. We talk to God when we worship Him. Simply put, we fellowship with God. Worshiping involves a personal revelation between God and man. When we pour out our inner thoughts to God, we use emotion to express our action. We might bow, we might kneel, or we may even lie on the floor. The Spirit will lead us to display our emotion.

Vincent and Maxine Brown

The pressures of everyday life can persuade us to focus on the here and now and thus forget God. Therefore, worship is so important. It takes our eyes off our current worries, gives us a glimpse of God's holiness, and allows us to look toward His future Kingdom.

The Value of Entering into the Holy of Holies
In the Book of Exodus, we learn that God chose Moses to lead His people out of Egypt. Moses led the people across the Red Sea to Mt. Sinai where a covenant was established between God and the Israelites. It was in this setting, according to Exodus 25, that God commanded Moses to build Him a sanctuary so that He could dwell among His people. God gave Moses specific instructions on the design and measurement of the tabernacle and its furnishings. While all the furnishings had a specific purpose, the Parochet-Veil separated the Holy Place from the Holy of Holies. As such, it symbolized the gulf that separated man from God. A sinful man is alienated from the presence of the living God. The veil not only symbolizes the separation between God and man but serves as a reminder that man needed a mediator to enable him to enter into God's presence.

Behind the veil, in the Holy of Holies, was the Ark of the Covenant, the most sacred article in the Tabernacle. There were three items inside the Ark of the Covenant: the golden pot of manna, Aaron's rod, and a copy of the law. On top of the Ark was the mercy seat that covered the law. The cherubim above the mercy seat represented God's reign over His people as Psalm

38

99:1 says: "The Lord reigns, let the people tremble! He sits enthroned upon the cherubim; let the people quake!" The value of entering the Holy of Holies became clear on the annual Day of Atonement. Once a year, the high priest went behind the veil and sprinkled blood upon the mercy seat once and on the east side of the Ark of the Covenant seven times as an act of expiation for the sins of his people, himself, and the priesthood. In the Ark of the Covenant was God's presence, His reign, His redemption, and His conversableness. God dwelt in His Shekinah glory in the Ark of the Covenant. However, when Christ was crucified, it is reported that the veil went from top to bottom. The tearing of the veil symbolized that the barrier that existed between God and man was eliminated, giving man the right to have access to God. The Scriptures tell us in Revelation 21:3, that the tabernacle of God is with men, and He will dwell with them, and they shall be His people, and God Himself shall be with them, and be their God.

The tabernacle in Hebrews serves as a model that we can follow today that will lead us into the actual presence of worship. The design of the tabernacle and the various articles of furniture demonstrate how a song service can lead worshipers into the presence of God. It begins in the outer court and ends in the Holy of Holies [the presence of God]. As we walk through the tabernacle, we take the three steps necessary for divine worship: thanksgiving, praise, and worship.

Chapter 10

How Do I Know that I am Saved?

In John 14:6, Jesus proclaimed that, "I AM THE WAY, THE TRUTH, AND THE LIFE. NO MAN COMETH UNTO THE FATHER BUT BY ME."

More than ten years ago, I accepted the Lord Jesus Christ as my personal Lord and Savior.

It was then that I was born again, or saved. I know that I am saved because I have faith and I believe in my heart that GOD'S Word is truth.

In 2 Corinthians 5:17, the Bible tells us, "THEREFORE, IF ANY MAN BE IN CHRIST HE IS A NEW CREATURE. OLD THINGS ARE PASSED AWAY, BEHOLD ALL THINGS ARE BECOME NEW. Romans 10:9-10 says, "THAT IF THOU

Vincent and Maxine Brown

SHALT CONFESS WITH THY MOUTH THE LORD JESUS, AND SHALT BELIEVE IN THINE HEART THAT GOD HATH RAISED HIM (JESUS CHRIST) FROM THE DEAD THOU SHALT BE SAVED."

The Bible tells us in 1 John 1:19, "THAT IF WE CONFESS OUR SINS, HE IS FAITHFUL AND JUST TO FORGIVE US OUR SINS AND CLEANSE US FROM ALL UNRIGHTEOUNESS."

I prayed the prayer of salvation when I accepted Jesus as Lord. I believed in my heart that Jesus Christ died for my sins and asked His forgiveness. I believe in Him as my crucified, buried, and risen Savior and asked Him to take charge of my life. With this act of faith, I became a member of the family of GOD, and the Body of Jesus Christ, and I was baptized by the Holy Spirit. To receive salvation, I had to repent, be truly sorry for my sins, and have a strong desire to make a change in my life and to serve Jesus Christ.

Having been raised in the Roman Catholic faith, I was never encouraged to study the Bible. Thus, I knew very little about the Word. When I joined The Church of St. Martin de Porres, I began attending Bible Study to learn more about GOD's Word. As I became more involved in the church ministries, I realized that I desired to become stronger and more knowledgeable about the Word of God. Consequently, to satisfy this need, I enrolled in Biblical Chronology at The Jericho Christian Training College.

Chapter 11

I Know What I Should Do but How Do I Do It?

In Romans 7-8, the Apostle Paul shows us that the law is powerless to save the sinner. Even though we take on a new nature, the law still condemns us because we are a slave to sin, and our sinful nature will always rebel against the law. Paul declares that salvation cannot be found by obeying the law. No matter who we are, only Jesus Christ can free us from sin. However, when we died with Christ on the Cross, the law no longer holds us in its power. When Christ was resurrected, we rose with Him as a new creature. As a result, we can produce good fruit, i.e., good deeds for God. We are able to do this because our renewed hearts and minds overflow with love for God, and He supplies the power for our Christian walk with Him.

The unbeliever has no relationship with God, so he taps his inner sources for power. However, he cannot earn salvation by obeying the ten commandments, attending church faithfully, or by doing good works. Without the help of Jesus, the unbeliever is overcome by sin, and cannot defend himself against its attacks. That is why we should never attempt to stand up against sin alone. Jesus Christ, who has conquered sin once and for all, promised to fight by our side. If we lean on Him, we will not have to give in to sin. The Law of Moses could not save us because of our sinful nature. But God put into effect a different plan. He sent His own Son to save us. God destroyed sin's control over us by giving His Son as a sacrifice for our sins. Since we are His children, we will share His treasures—for everything God gives His Son is also ours. But if we share in His glory, we must also share in His suffering.

Chapter 12

If God Were to Go on Strike

In Ephesians 1:3, Paul writes: "Blessed be the God and Father of our Lord Jesus Christ, who hath blessed us with all spiritual blessings in heavenly places in Christ." This means all the good things God gives us—salvation, the gifts of the Spirit, power to do God's will, the hope of living forever with Christ—we can enjoy these blessings now. In Verse 4, Paul continues: "According as He hath chosen us in Him before the foundation of the world, that we should be holy and without blame before Him in love." Paul said that God has chosen us to emphasize that salvation depends totally on God. We are not saved because we deserve it, but because God is gracious and gives grace freely according to His plan. Through predestination, God has adopted us as His own children. Through Jesus' sacrifice, He brought us into His family and made us joint heirs with Jesus. In other words, we now belong to Jesus Christ.

Throughout the Bible, God has revealed Himself through Holy scripture. He revealed Himself to us most perfectly in Jesus Christ. John 14:9 reads: "He that hath seen Jesus has seen the Father." In Romans 5:8-10 it says, "God demonstrates His infinite love for us, in that while we were yet sinners, Christ died for us. Having now been justified by His blood, we shall be saved from the wrath of God through Jesus. For while we were enemies, we were reconciled to God and saved through the death and resurrection of His Son."

According to Hebrews 13;5, God promised that "I will never leave you nor will I ever forsake you." This is because God has sealed us with His Holy Spirit. THE HOLY SPIRIT IS GOD HIMSELF. In John 6:37-39, Jesus said: "All that the Father giveth me shall come to me, and him that cometh to me I will in no way cast out. For I came down from heaven, not to do mine own will, but the will of Him that sent me. And this is the Father's will which hath sent me, that of all He hath given me I should lose nothing but should rise up again at the last day." Jesus did not work independently of the Father, but in union with Him. This gives us even more assurance of being welcomed into His presence and being protected by Him. In Verse 39, Jesus said that He would not lose even one person that the Father had given Him. Therefore, anyone who makes a sincere commitment to believe in Jesus Christ as Savior is secure in God's promise of eternal life.

The scenario suggested in the title of this chapter is of no consequence to God's children. If by chance God were to go on strike, this would mean that Jesus, and the Holy Spirit would also go on strike since they are one, and we would perish without them. God's Word assures us that He will never leave us nor forsake us. In John 6:39, Jesus further assures us that He would not lose even one person that the Father hath given Him. By trusting faith, and by being humble and obedient, we are assured that God would not go on strike. The Holy Scripture reveals to us more about God than human reasoning could ever teach us. We know that God's Word is truth, and it is more important for us to believe His Word than to understand it.

Chapter 13

Jehovah-Jireh, the Lord Will Provide

In Genesis 22:2-14, God commanded Abraham to take his only son Isaac to the land of Moriah and offer him as a burnt offering. Without hesitation, Abraham began preparing himself and Isaac for the journey to Mt. Moriah. Upon their arrival to the appointed place, Isaac noticed his father had wood and a fire for the burnt offering, but no lamb. When Isaac questioned his father about the lamb, Abraham answered—God will provide Himself a lamb for a burnt offering. When they came to the appointed place, Abraham prepared an altar and prepared to slay his son. God stopped Abraham and provided him with a ram for a burnt offering instead of Isaac. As a memorial, Abraham named that place Jehovah-Jireh.

God was really testing Abraham's obedience. He had no intention of accepting Isaac as a burnt offering. In fact, God condemned the heathen practice of human sacrifice. God's purpose for testing Abraham was to strengthen his character, Genesis 22:7,8. Through this difficult experience, Abraham strengthened his commitment to God. He also learned of God's ability to always provide. Obeying God is often a struggle because it may mean giving up something or someone we really like.

There is a close relationship between the ram offered on the altar as a substitute for Isaac and Jesus Christ offered on the Cross as a substitute for us. Whereas God stopped Abraham from sacrificing his son, God did not spare His own Son Jesus from dying on the Cross. If Jesus had lived, the rest of humankind would have died. God sent His only Son to die for us so that we can be spared from eternal death and instead receive eternal life, John 3:16.

Chapter 14

Jesus' Mission, Our Mission

When Adam sinned back in the Garden of Eden, three things happened to him. He became spiritually separated from God, he could no longer communicate with God, and he no longer had any knowledge of God. Adam's sin affected the whole human race. In fact, ever since then, every human was born into the world in a state of sin. God is holy and perfect; therefore, He cannot associate with anyone who has sin in his life. Without God, we are lost. John 3:16 assures us that God so loved the world that He gave His only begotten Son, that whoever believes in Him shall not perish but have everlasting life. I Peter 3:18 reveals that Christ suffered once for sins, the just for the unjust that He might bring us to God.

Jesus' overall mission was to come into the world to preach the Gospel of repentance to save men from their sins that they should never perish. Matthew 28:18 tells us that God gave Jesus the authority over Heaven and Earth. Jesus' mission was prophesied in Isaiah 61. In Luke 4:18, we find Jesus reading to the people, and quoting the words found in Isaiah 61:1, which read: "The Spirit of the Lord is upon Me, Because He hath anointed Me to preach the gospel to the poor; He hath sent me to heal the broken hearted, to preach deliverance to the captives, and recovering of sight to the blind, to set at liberty them that are bruised." It is important to understand that everything Jesus did was under the anointing of the Holy Spirit. On the basis of the authority that God passed on to Jesus, He (Jesus) gave His disciples the Great Commission. The disciples, working in the power of the Holy Spirit, would carry the Gospel of God's Kingdom out of Palestine and into the whole world. Jesus told them to make more disciples as they preached, baptized, and taught. With this same authority, Jesus still commands all believers to tell others the Gospel and make them disciples of the Kingdom.

As born-again Christians, the Holy Spirit indwells in all believers as their enabler, and works in their hearts in such a way that they magnify the person of Jesus. God sees us as joint heirs with His Son Jesus. Our mission is to take His Gospel message throughout the world. In John 14:12,13, Jesus proclaimed: "He that believes in Me, and the works that I do, he shall do also; and greater works than these shall he do because I go unto my Father—And whatever you ask in My Name, that will I do, that My Father will be glorified in the Son." When Jesus was on Earth, He traveled only a short distance from His hometown. Thus, Jesus' message only reached those within the confines in which He traveled.

When Jesus ascended on High, He commissioned all believers to witness on His behalf; the indwelling of the Holy Spirit made it possible for His Church (Body of Christ) to take God's message worldwide. To help us successfully carry out this mission, Jesus gave ministry gifts to the Church. These gifts were for the perfecting of the Saints, for the work of the ministry, and for edifying the body of Christ.

Chapter 15

Miracles in My Life

As I reflect back over the years, I recall a period in my life that I will refer to as my *wilderness experience*. Since I began studying at Jericho, I have learned that our obedience to God, or lack thereof, will determine how long we remain in our wilderness experience. During this period of my life, I encountered some difficulties which could have been fatal had it not been for the grace of God. I was involved in two major car accidents. In the first major accident, my car was completely demolished. I had fallen asleep, and I struck several parked cars and a telephone pole, which snapped in half and fell across my car. The car was so badly twisted that the glove compartment was resting just inches from my right arm. The only area not crushed was the space where I was sitting. I only suffered minor injuries.

In the second accident, I was driving at night in rainy weather when another vehicle pulled in front of me. I was driving too fast for the road conditions, which caused me to collide with the rear of the vehicle. My car was totaled. Although I was knocked unconscious, my injuries were minor.

In the third accident, I was swimming at Cape May, New Jersey. I swam out a good distance from the beach home and I became tired. When I attempted to stand up to rest, I did not realize that the tide had come in which made the water deeper. Consequently, I panicked and began to take on water. I was too tired to swim back to shore and I was choking from the water that I had swallowed. As I was thrashing about in the water, a voice told me to turn on my back, which I did immediately. Then, I recalled having learned to float on my back when I was a boy scout. I immediately regained my confidence and strength and swam back to shore. I believe that God continues to perform miracles as He deems necessary to bring His believers back in line with His Word.

Chapter 16

Satan's Ten Deceptions

Religious Deception (Ritualistic), Matthew 6:2. The term hypocrite, as used in Matthew, means a person who does good acts for appearance only. These empty acts are his only reward. God will reward only those who are sincere in their faith.

Doctrinal Deception (Access the Bible as allegorical, not the truth). Matthew 22:29. The Sadducees asked Jesus what marriage would be like in Heaven. Jesus said it was more important to understand God's power than to know what Heaven will be like. In every generation and culture, ideas of eternal life seem to be based upon images and experiences of present life. Jesus answered that these faulty ideas are caused by ignorance of God's Word. We should concentrate more on our relationship with God.

Ethical Deception (Only being a Christian because it seems ethically right), Matthew 12:33. This is descriptive of a Sunday Christian—one who shows up because it is politically correct to do so. They think of it as a religious duty, rather than honoring God. Others perform good deeds or work in church ministries, not to glorify Christ, but to seek special recognition.

Moral Deception (If you want to do it do it, otherwise, do as you feel morally right), 1 Corinthians 6:19. When we become Christians, the Holy Spirit lives within us. Therefore, we no longer own our bodies and have no right to defile our bodies as we wish.

1 Corinthians 6:20. We have been "bought" with a price refers to slaves purchased at auction. Christ's death freed us from sin, but also obligates us to His service. If you live in a building owned by someone else, you do not violate the rules of the building. Because our bodies belong to God, we must honor Him and live by His standards.

Intellectual Deception (Everyone's view is equal and acceptable), Proverbs 3:5. When we have to make an important decision, sometimes we feel like we cannot trust anyone—not even God. However, God is a better judge of what we want and need than we are! We must trust Him completely in every choice we make.

Proverbs 3:6. To receive God's guidance said Solomon, we must acknowledge God in all that we do. We need to look at our values and priorities and determine where God is on our list. We must make God a vital part of everything we do, then He will guide us toward accomplishing His purposes.

Fanatical Deception (Doing crazy things under the guise of religion), John 8:44. Jesus made a distinction between hereditary sons and true sons. The religious leaders were hereditary sons of Abraham and, therefore, claimed to be sons of God. But their actions showed them to be true sons of Satan, for they lived under Satan's guidance. Their hatred of truth, their lies, and their murderous intentions indicated how much control Satan had over them. True sons of Abraham (faithful followers of God) would not function as they did. Your church membership and family connections will not make you true sons of God.

Mystical Deception (Visions, voices, dreams), Matthew 12:39. In Matthew 12:38-40, the Pharisees were asking Jesus for another miracle, but they were not sincerely seeking to know Jesus. Jesus knew that they had already seen enough miraculous proof to convince them that He was the Messiah if they would just open their hearts. Many people have thought, if I could only see a miracle, then I could really believe in God. But Jesus' response to the Pharisees applies to us. We have plenty of evidence—Jesus' death, resurrection, His ascension, and centuries of His work in the lives of believers around the world. We should accept what God has already given and move on.

Sexual Deception (If it is permissive to engage in sex if neither party is married or if you are in the process of divorce),

Hebrews 13:4. To guard against sexual immorality, God has ordained the sacred relationship of marriage. Undefiled contains more than an approval of a conjugal relationship, but also entails the married couples' responsibility to preserve their intimacy from the perverse and debasing practices of lewd society.

Galatians 5:16. The Fruit of the Spirit is the spontaneous of the Holy Spirit in us. The Spirit produces these character traits, which are found in the nature of Christ. Thus, being led by the Spirit involves the desire to hear, the readiness to obey God, and the sensitivity to discern between your feelings and His promptings. Then, the words of Christ will be in your mind, the love of Christ in your actions, and the power of Christ will help you control your selfish desires.

Spiritual Deception (Becoming bored with Christian life, always looking for a thrill), Romans 8:1. The "flesh," as used throughout this chapter, refers not to our human bodies, but to the principle and power of sin. Sin is present and often operating in our body, but not to be equated with the body.

Philippians 4:8. What we put into our minds determines what comes out in our words and actions. Paul tells us to program our minds with thoughts that are true, honest, just, pure, lovely, good report, virtuous, and praiseworthy Replace harmful material with wholesome material and read God's Word, and pray asking for help in focusing your mind on what is good and pure.

Failure to 'Bury Your Past" Deception (Allowing life's mistakes to plague you), Luke 9:62. Jesus wants total dedication, not half-hearted commitment. We cannot pick and choose among Jesus' ideas and follow Him selectively; we must accept the Cross along with the Crown, Judgement as well as Mercy. We must continue to focus on Jesus.

Revelation 21:8. The "fearful" are not those who are faint-hearted in their faith or who sometimes doubt or question, but those who turn back from following God. They are not brave enough to stand up for Christ; they are not humbled enough to accept His authority over their lives. They are put on the same list as the unrepentant, abominable, murderers, liars, idolaters, the immoral, and those practicing demonic arts.

Chapter 17

Stewardship of Our Time

What should be our prayer concerning the use of our time that God gives us? Psalms 90:12 says we should pray as Moses did in Verse 12 and ask God to teach us to number our days. Realizing that our time is short on planet Earth, we should ask God to give us wisdom to use our time wisely. We need to draw closer to God through prayer, and by being obedient to His Word. We should try to develop a Christ-like character, and to use our God-given talents and gifts to serve others.

What does God demand of us in the stewardship of our time? Psalms 62:8 says, "When do you find this hardest to do?" God demands us to be faithful and committed in the stewardship of our time. In other words, our time is God's time, and we must manage our time as God commanded and not allow disobedience to keep us from bearing fruit.

What does Christ admonish us to do as stewards of our time until He returns? Mark 13:33-37 tells us, "Jesus admonishes us to take heed, watch, and pray for no one knows the day or the hour." We should study God's Word and tell others about Christ while we wait for His return. We must live by His instructions each day and pray to the Holy Spirit for wisdom and understanding. In Verse 37, Jesus tells all to *Watch!*

What is necessary in order to know fully the will of God concerning the duties of our stewardship? Ephesians 5:18 says, we should submit daily to the leading of the Holy Spirit, and draw on His power to help us understand the stewardship role.

In whose name should the steward perform these duties? Colossians 3:17 says, "Whatever we do in word or deed, do it in the name of the Lord Jesus, giving thanks to God the Father through Him."

As with wise stewards who know and are obedient to the will of God, what will we spend much of our time aggressively doing? Mark 16:15 says, "Preaching the Gospel to every creature throughout all the world."

Chapter 18

The Book of Matthew, He is the Messiah

The purpose of Matthew's Gospel is to prove to his fellow Jews that Jesus was truly the Messiah, the eternal King. Matthew begins his book by showing how Jesus Christ was a descendant of King David. Matthew explains that God did not send Jesus to be an earthly King, but a heavenly King. His Kingdom would be much greater than David's because it would never end. Even at His birth, many recognized Jesus as King. They worshiped Him and brought Him royal gifts. We must be willing to recognize Jesus for who He really is and worship Him as King of our lives.

Matthew tells of Jesus' birth and early years, including the family's flight to Egypt to escape Herod. At Jesus' baptism, He was identified as the Messiah (John 1:29-34). Jesus did not begin His public ministry until after He had demonstrated His ability to overcome the temptation of Satan. He then called His disciples

Vincent and Maxine Brown

together and preached the Sermon on the Mount (Matthew 5:3-10. He taught the Beatitudes, which presented a set of values that Jesus expects His followers to adopt, because they are important to God. These are not the values most people think of as important. Throughout Jesus' public ministry, He performed miracles of healing the sick, the demon possessed, and raising the dead. Despite opposition from the Pharisees and others in the religious establishment, He continued to teach concerning the Kingdom of Heaven. He preached about forgiveness, peace, and putting others first. These characteristics make one great in the Kingdom of God. Jesus was truly the Messiah, the One for whom the Jews had waited to deliver them from Roman oppression, yet tragically, they did not recognize Him when He came because His Kingship was not what they expected. The true purpose of God's anointed Deliverer was to die for all people to free them from sin's oppression. Jesus came to Earth to begin His Kingdom. His full Kingdom will be realized when He returns and will be made up of all who faithfully followed Him.

The way to enter God's Kingdom is by faith—believing in Christ to save us from sin and change our lives. When we have faith in Jesus Christ, the magnitude of God's love is total. His love reaches every corner of our experience and continues for the length of our lives. The power of the Holy Spirit helps us to live morally renewed and regenerated lives. If we are to receive all that God has predestined for us, Jesus wants our total dedication, not a half-hearted commitment. We must be willing to abandon everything that has given us security, and focus on Jesus. We must be obedient and allow nothing to distract us from Godly living. As we can see, God's love surpasses all understanding. He not only allowed His Son to die for our sins, but through His shed blood, He took on our infirmities. True believers gain eternal life, with all its treasures, by acknowledging Christ as Lord and Savior, and recognizing His saving work, and by identifying with the Christian community. We have the fullness of the Holy Spirit, and He continually renews our hearts. None of this occurs because we earned it or deserve it, it is all a gift of God's Grace.

Chapter 19

The Hand of God

As I reflect back over my life, I realize just how God has blessed me and protected me all of my life. I was the oldest of six children, two sisters and three brothers. My parents were devout Roman Catholics which meant I, too, was brought up as a Roman Catholic. Our family was relatively poor, and it was difficult to make ends meet. Consequently, when I reached school age, I went to live with my father's sister. This arrangement offered me two significant benefits. First, it shielded me from the hardships that my brothers and sisters experienced. Second, I was encouraged to participate in religious activities at church. For several years, I taught Sunday School classes and later became certified to teach high school religion. I also served as principal of our church Sunday school. After a while, I became disillusioned with the church doctrine, and I decided that religion was not for me. I needed more; I needed something that would give me hope. Let me explain!

We were taught that Roman Catholicism was God's chosen religion, as such, we were not allowed to participate in the worship service of any other denomination. Non-Catholics were prohibited from receiving Holy Communion, and we were not allowed to participate in Holy Communion until we confessed our sins to the priest. The priest was our intercessor and had the power to absolve sins. He would then pronounce your penance. Penance usually consisted of reciting repetitive prayers to the virgin Mary and reciting the Lord's Prayer. I don't recall repentance being an option. We were never encouraged to read the Bible. Instead, we were taught from the Catechism of the Catholic Church. Much emphasis was placed on worshiping the virgin Mary as opposed to having a personal relationship with the Lord Jesus. In retrospect, I can see that many of our teachings were ritualistic and some of the practices were derived from the Old Testament times. This included the Ten Commandments, which I found impossible to keep. So, I decided to drop out of the race.

Over the next ten years, I sort of placed God on a shelf, and I began to live my life of destruction. First, I focused on advancing my career. I rapidly climbed the ladder and achieved much success. I became the first African American in my agency to be promoted to various key positions of power. This is when I really lost focus on God, and I began to gravitate toward other people who had the same goals, or who had become disillusioned with life as I had. I quickly learned that without God's hedge of protection around us, we pay a heavy price. I became accident prone. I was involved in two major accidents, as I explained earlier, where both cars were completely demolished, yet God spared my life. I was plagued with chronic illnesses, and I was hospitalized twice. I nearly lost my job, but God gave me the wisdom to overcome this adversity. I finally became separated from my family, which ultimately ended in divorce.

During this period, God began to place Godly people in my life, and they inspired me to change my direction and return to God. I found a Bible teaching church, attended Bible study, and became involved in the Ministry of Helps. Eight years later, I had developed a burning desire to learn more about the Holy Scriptures. I was directed toward *Maple Springs Bible College*. However, on the day of registration, I heard a radio announcement that *Jericho's Christian College* was holding open house. God led me to the right place to receive the meat of the Word that was being taught by anointed teachers. Final report, I have become a vessel that God has used in mighty ways. I no longer suffer from chronic illnesses. I have not been involved in anymore automobile accidents and I have not been hospitalized. I am remarried to a very supportive wife who constantly encourages me to continue my studies. Finally, I was able to retire in 1996 with forty years of government service.

Chapter 20

The Lord's Blood-Stained Clothing

Here is the question. Will the blood flow six feet deep as stated in Revelation 14:20, or did the blood spatter six feet high according to Isaiah 63:3? The referenced scriptures are as follows:

Revelation 14-20, and the winepress was trampled outside the city, and blood came out of the winepress, up to the horse's bridle, for one thousand, six hundred furlongs.

Isaiah 63:3, I have trampled the winepress alone: And from the Nations no one was with me. I trampled them in my anger (fury), and the blood spattered (sprinkled) my garments and I stained all my clothes.

In Revelation 14:14, the harvest is about to take place. Jesus appears in John's vision wearing a crown of gold—symbolizing He is King of Kings—He carries a sharp sickle that He uses to harvest grain (the Gentiles), and grapes (the unbelieving Jews), and the unrepentant sinners of the tribulation. This is an image of judgement: Christ is separating the faithful from the unfaithful like a farmer harvesting crops. In Lamentations 1:15, Jeremiah proclaimed: "The Lord has trampled underfoot all my mighty men in my midst. He has called an assembly against me to crush my young men. The Lord trampled as in a winepress."

The scriptures tell us that the blood reached the horses bridle and spattered the Lord's clothing as well. In Revelation 14, we know that blood came out of the winepress up to the horses bridle for 1,600 furlongs. This is 180 miles long. In Isaiah, the Lord proclaimed that He trampled the unrepentant sinners in such anger and fury that their blood spattered His garments and stained all His clothing.

The winepress used in the Bible is symbolic of God's wrath and judgement against sin. In speaking of God's wrath, one would surmise that in anger He rode the horse at a very fast pace which would explain the spattering upward because the horse-shoes would throw the blood quite high. Blood flowed out of the press in such volume and force that the Lord became soaked and spattered from all directions.

Chapter 21

The Prayer of Jabez

Now Jabez was more honorable than his brothers, and his mother called his name saying,

"Because I bore him in pain." And Jabez called on the God of Israel saying, "Oh that you would bless me indeed and enlarge my territory, that Your hand would be with me and that You would keep me from evil, that I might not cause pain! So God granted him what he requested."

Jabez is remembered for a prayer, rather than a heroic act. In his prayer, he asked God to (1) bless him, (2) help him in his work, (3) be with him in all that he did, and (4) keep him from evil and disaster. Jabez acknowledged God as the true center of his work. When we pray for God's blessing, we should also pray that He will take His rightful position as Lord over our work, our family time, and our recreation. Obeying Him in our daily responsibilities is heroic living.

Jabez prayed specifically for God to protect him from evil and disaster. We live in a fallen world where sin abounds, and it is important to ask God to keep us safe from unavoidable evils that come our way. But we must also avoid evil motives, desires, and actions that begin within us. Therefore, we must not only seek God's protection from evil, but we must also ask God to guard our thoughts and actions. We can begin to use His protection by filling our minds with positive thoughts and attitudes.

Chapter 22

The Relevance of the Tabernacle to My Life

Where It All Began—In Genesis 3, God promised the coming Savior—hundreds of years earlier God had already planned to defeat Satan and offer salvation to the world through His Son, Jesus Christ. Because of the sin of Adam and Eve, sin was rampant throughout the world. People refused to obey God. Consequently, God decided to destroy the world with a great flood. Noah and his family were the only inhabitants who still worshiped God. Because of Noah's faithfulness and obedience, God chose him to build an Ark. When he and his family were safely inside the Ark, the great flood came and destroyed all life on Earth. Many years passed. Jacob and his children were all dead. But their descendants still lived in Egypt. Pharaoh enslaved the people of Israel for 400 years. He oppressed them cruelly. They prayed for deliverance from this cruel system. God answered their prayers through His mighty miracles and through the leadership of Moses. Moses led them out of Egypt to the Promised Land. God initiated the annual Passover celebration as a reminder of their escape from slavery. God also rescues us from the slavery of sin. The Lord Jesus Christ celebrated the Passover with His disciples at the "Last Supper' and then went on to rescue us from sin by dying for us on the Cross.

The Wilderness Experience—those who travel, move, or face new challenges know what it is to be uprooted. Life is full of changes and few things remain stable. The Israelites were constantly moving through the wilderness toward Canaan (Numbers 11-21). God was clearly present with the Israelites. His pillar of cloud and fire led them; His manna fed them daily. But, instead of being grateful, they grumbled and complained. They were only able to survive the rigorous journey because of God's presence and His trustworthy guidance. In Exodus 15:22, Moses and his brother Aaron, Israel's first High Priest, brought Israel from the Red Sea into the wilderness. They would praise and worship God one day but would complain to Him the next day. First, they complained of not having water. When they later found water in Marah, they complained of its bitterness, so they could not drink it. They then turned their complaints against Moses. He cried out to the Lord and the Lord showed Moses a tree. When he cast it into the waters, the waters became sweet. Throughout the journey, the Israelites continued to complain. In Numbers 11:4-10, we learn that every morning the Israelites pulled back the tent doors and witnessed a miracle. Covering the ground was white fluffy manna—food from Heaven. But they soon complained that was not enough. Believing it was their right to have more, they forgot what God had already blessed them with. They didn't ask God to fill their need, instead they demanded meat and stopped trusting God to care for them. They complained to Moses as they reminisced about the good food they had in Egypt.

God gave them what they asked for, but because of their sinful attitude, He punished them by sending a plague. In Numbers 11:1-15, the Israelites complained and then Moses complained. But God responded positively to Moses and negatively to the Israelites. The people complained to one another, and nothing was accomplished. Moses took his complaint to God who can solve any problem. Some of us are good at complaining to each other. Like the Israelites, we, too, go through our own personal *wilderness experience.* Our time in the wilderness is up to us before we get to the Promised Land. However, the time we spend in the wilderness prepares us for loftier heights. When we feel like complaining, we must learn to take our problems to God in prayer, because complaining only extends our time in the wilderness, and elevates our feeling of stress. Prayer quiets our thoughts and emotions and prepares us to listen to God. Matthew 10:30 says that "God is greatly interested in us." We should not be afraid to talk with Him about any of our concerns—no matter how small or how unimportant they may seem to us. We must also remember that when we ask God for something, He may grant our request. But, if we approach Him with a sinful attitude, getting what we want may prove costly.

Israel at Mount Sinai—With God's help, Moses and the Israelites arrived at Mount Sinai after escaping through the Red Sea, and wandering in the wilderness for almost 40 years. Mount Sinai was one of the most sacred locations in Israel's history. This mountain is where Moses met God in the burning bush and where God made His covenant with Israel. Because of the Israelites' disobedience and constant complaining, they failed to see that their wanderings in the wilderness were a direct result of their parents' sins, as well as their own disobedience. Even though God guided them in a cloud by day and fire by night, the Israelites could not accept the fact that they brought their problems upon themselves, so they blamed Moses for their condition. Oftentimes, our troubles result from our own disobedience or lack of faith. Until we face reality that we must trust God completely, there will be little peace and no spiritual growth in our lives.

When God finally called Moses up to the mountain top, He gave him the Ten Commandments, additional laws to guide the Israelites to live righteously, and a blueprint for building a portable Tabernacle where the people could worship and offer sacrifices to God. Moses met with God for so long that the people grew impatient and began to lose faith in God. Consequently, they urged Aaron to make an idol in the form of a golden calf, so they could worship it instead of the Living God. Many of them broke the first commandment and worshiped the idol, giving it credit for freeing them from slavery. God had already warned His people to avoid false religions and false gods. Consequently, He punished those who were guilty, as the Covenant Law specified that He should.

Through Israel's experience at Mount Sinai, we learn about the importance of obedience in our relationship with God. His laws help expose sin, and they give us standards for righteous living. The laws are also necessary because everything we do has positive or negative consequences. It is vital to think before acting in order to consider the effect of our choices. As we relate with others, we should keep the principles of these laws in mind. We should act responsibly and justly with all people—friend and enemies alike. In spite of the fact that the Israelites broke God's law, He remained faithful to His promise to Abraham that Israel would become a Holy Nation, a Kingdom of priests in which anyone could approach God freely.

It didn't take long, however, for the people to corrupt God's plan. When they reached the borders of Canaan, Moses sent out men to explore the land. The men reported that the land was fertile, but that Canaan's inhabitants were powerful and their fortified cities frightening. Terrified by the report, the Israelites refused to obey God's command to attack and take the Promised Land. Direct disobedience to God called for punishment. Moses prayed for the people, and God pardoned their sin. But the Israelites could not avoid the consequences of their willingness to disobey God. Until the entire generation of those who were unwilling to obey had died out, the Israelites were forced to wander in the wilderness... waiting. The new generation of

Israelite was about to enter the Promised Land when Moses reminded them of all that God had done for them. He summarized the way God's people were to live in order to enjoy His blessing.

However, with the coming of Jesus Christ, God has once again extended His covenant to all believers including the Gentiles. We are to become a "royal priesthood" (1 Peter 2:9). The death and resurrection of Jesus Christ has allowed each of us to approach God freely without an intermediary. There is no need for us to wait once a year to have our sins forgiven. We can ask God's forgiveness at any time or place.

God's Directions for Building the Tabernacle—Exodus 25-31 records God's directions to Moses for building the tabernacle. Chapters 35-39 tell how these instructions were to be carried out. The instructions were specific. Each detail of the Tabernacle God taught a different spiritual truth. For instance, the high quality of the precious materials making up the Tabernacle show God's greatness and transcendence. The Book of Matthew 25:51 describes the Temple as having three main parts—the courts, the Holy Place (where only the priests could enter), and the Holy of Holies where only the High Priest could enter. The High Priest entered only once a year, to atone for the sins of the Nation. In Leviticus 16:1 35, we learn that the curtain separating the Holy Place from the Holy of Holies was split in two upon the death of Christ. The splitting of the curtain was a symbol that the barrier between God and man was removed.

Now, all people were free to approach God. The veil surrounding the "Most Holy Place" shows God's moral perfection from the common and the unclean.

The portable nature of the Tabernacle allowed the people to worship God daily, and enabled God to be with His people as they traveled through the wilderness. Finally, God instructed that there be only one door leading to the worship center to show that there is only one way to approach God—His way.

Furniture for the Tabernacle—The book of Exodus describes furniture placed in the Tabernacle. The Ark of the Testimony was the most sacred of all the furniture. Here, the Hebrews kept a copy of the Ten Commandments which summarized the whole covenant. The priest had to be pure to enter the presence of God, so they used the Brass Laver for cleansing. The Altar of Burnt Offering was used for animal sacrifices, and was located in the court in front of the Tabernacle. The Golden Candlestick stood in the holy place, opposite the table of shewbread. The Table of Shewbread was a stand on which the offerings were placed. In the presence of God, there were always 12 loaves of fresh bread on the table representing the 12 tribes. Inside the Tabernacle was the Altar of Incense. The incense burned on the altar was a perfume of sweet-smelling aroma where the holy anointing oil was made. Moses and his people followed God's instructions in every minute detail. God was keenly interested and concerned about even the little things.

In Exodus 39-42, we learn that Moses exercised his management skills well. He gave important responsibilities to others and then trusted them to do the job. Great leaders like Moses give plans and directions while letting others participate on the team. If you are a leader, consider trusting your assistants with key responsibilities. When Moses inspected the finished work, he saw that it was done the way God wanted and blessed the people. A good leader follows up on assigned tasks and gives rewards for good work. In whatever responsible position you find yourself in, follow up to make sure that the assigned tasks are completed as intended, and show your appreciation to the people who have assisted you. In Numbers 10:29-32, we find Moses complimenting Hobab and his wilderness skills. Moses let him know that his assistance was needed and appreciated. People cannot know that you appreciate them if you don't tell them that they are important to you. Complimenting those who deserve it builds lasting relationships and helps people know that they are truly valued.

The Relevance of the Tabernacle to our Lives—God recruited Moses to build the Tabernacle and Moses delegated many important responsibilities to his assistants in order to complete the task. He assigned tasks based on his assessment of the skills and abilities of his people. God also allows us, as believers, to participate with Him in carrying out His will. Our job is not to just sit and watch God's chosen leaders work, but to give our best efforts when work needs to be done. In Exodus 40:17-33, we learn that the physical care of the Tabernacle required the completion of a long list of tasks important to the work of God's house. This principle is important for us to remember today when God's house is the Church. There are many seemingly unimportant tasks to be carried out to maintain our church building. Cleaning, maintenance, and repair work may not seem very spiritual, but the work is vital to the ministry of the Church and to God. In fact, any ability or capacity we have, when used to glorify God and encourage others, becomes a spiritual gift. Our gifts may not be named on any list, but we'll recognize them as coming from God when others tell us that what we do draws them closer to God. So, use the one thing you do well to glorify God today.

In Exodus 28-1, we see that in order for God to teach His people how to worship Him, He needed ministers to oversee the operation of the Tabernacle and help the people maintain their relationship with God. These men were called priests and Levites, and they could be members only of the tribe of Levi. The priests were also descendants of Aaron, Israel's first "High Priest." As High Priest, Aaron was responsible for the activities of the priests and the Levites and as High Priest, he wore a breastplate. The symbolism of the breastplate reminds us that we have a two-way relationship with God. The breastplate featured precious stones engraved with the names of the twelve tribes of Israel.

Each time the High Priest ministered in the Tabernacle or Temple; he symbolically spoke to God for all the people. The priests performed the daily sacrifices, maintained the Tabernacle, and counseled the people on how to be holy and follow God. They were the people's representatives before God and thus were required to live lives worthy of their office. The Lord Jesus is now our High Priest (Hebrews 8). Daily sacrifices are no longer required because Jesus made the ultimate sacrifice Himself when He died on the Cross for our sins. Today, we speak to God directly to praise Him and to communicate our needs and God responds to us through Heaven's best. He gives us His walking Word, His printed Word, His indwelling Word, the five-fold ministries, and 72,000 angels to watch over us. Ministers today no longer sacrifice animals. Instead, they lead us in prayer and teach us about both the benefits and the commandments that characterize our new life as Christians.

The Tabernacle was God's home on Earth (Exodus 40:34). He filled it with His glory and overpowering sense of presence. Almost 500 years later, Solomon built the Temple which replaced the Tabernacle as the central place of worship. God also filled the Temple with His glory (2 Chronicles 5:13,14). But when Israel again turned from God, His glory and presence departed from the Temple, and it was destroyed by invading armies. The Temple was later rebuilt, and God's glory returned in even greater splendor five centuries later when Jesus Christ, God's Son, entered the Temple and taught.

When Jesus was crucified, God's glory again left the Temple. However, God no longer needed a physical building after

Jesus rose from the dead. God's Temple is now His Church, the Body of Believers. God dwells in us by His Spirit. Because of Jesus' perfect sacrifice, there is no longer a need for further priests and sacrifices. In comparison, the old agreement was the covenant law between God and Israel. The new and better way is the covenant of grace, which is Christ's offer to forgive our sins and bring us to God through His sacrificial death. This agreement is new, and it extends beyond Israel and Judah to all the Gentile Nations. It is new in application because it is written in our hearts and minds. It offers a new way to forgiveness, not through animal sacrifices, but through the blood of Jesus.

The life and ministry of Moses shows us how salvation for many is found through one man. Like Jesus, Moses was chosen and cared for by God. Like Jesus, Moses' special ministry was to save God's people from death. The Lord Jesus Christ saves us from spiritual death and gives us eternal life if we become and remain a part of God's family. Jesus is not only our Savior, but He is also our High Priest who sits at the right hand of God as our Intercessor.

Chapter 23

Time is of the Essence

Our Prophetic Future— "When He (Christ) Returns
for His Church, Will We Be Ready"

When man sinned back in the Garden of Eden, three things
happened to him: (1) he became dead to God; (2) he lost com-
munication with God; and (3) he no longer had knowledge of
God. God so loved us that He made provisions for our redemption. John 3:16 says, "For God so loved the world that He gave
His only begotten Son, that whoever believes in Him should not
perish but have everlasting life."

In the Book of Acts, the four Gospels reveal the last recorded
facts about Jesus. The Book of Matthew addresses the Resurrection of Jesus. Mark speaks about the Ascension; the Book of
Luke reveals the promise of the Holy Spirit, and the Book of
John predicted the second coming of the Lord Jesus Christ. Acts
1 brings all four Gospels together. This is the age of the coming
of the Holy Spirit, and the inspired record of the beginnings of

the Church. The importance of this age is the indwelling of the Holy Spirit (1Corinthians 6:19). These truths were foretold by God, the first three truths have come to pass. Therefore, we must be mindful that God's timetable is not our timetable and remember that "Time is of the Essence."

In Ephesians, the Church is revealed as God's masterpiece. It is more wonderful than any temple made with hands, constructed of living stones, and indwelt by the Holy Spirit (2:20-22). It is the Body of Christ in the world—to walk as He would walk and to wrestle against the whiles of the devil (1:22,23; 4:1; 6:11,12). Ephesians addresses all churches regardless of geography, for the Church is "one body" and its location "is in the heavenlies." God the Father planned the Church, and God the Son paid the price for the Church through His blood. Thus, God will return for His Church. In 3:6, the Holy Spirit revealed that we, the Gentiles, are fellow heirs of the same body as the apostles and prophets and are partakers of His promise in Christ through the Gospel. When Christ returns for His Church, only spiritual Christians will be raptured.

In Thessalonians 5:16-17 it reads, "For the Lord Himself will descend from the heavens. And the dead in Christ will rise first. Then we who are alive and remain shall be caught up together with them in the clouds to meet the Lord in the air. And we shall always be with the Lord." Will We be Ready?

The Great Tribulation will last for a period of seven years. Scripture indicates that this period will be characterized by judgment, wrath, trial, darkness, desolation, overturning, and punishment. The Nations will be judged for their sin and rejection of Christ. The final "week" of seven years will begin for Israel when the Antichrist confirms a "covenant" of seven years (Daniel 9:27). When this peace pact is signed, this will signal the beginning of the tribulation period. That signature marks the beginning of the seven-year countdown to the Second Coming of Christ (which follows the Tribulation period). Will We Be Ready— "Time is of the Essence."

Chapter 24

Why I Need to be Filled with the Holy Spirit

On the last night when Jesus was with His disciples, He promised to send the Holy Spirit as their Comforter. Although Jesus' bodily presence was removed, the Holy Spirit would so reveal Christ in the hearts of the disciples, that they would experience His presence with them continually. We need to be filled with the Holy Spirit also, because it is God's desire to have a continual fellowship with His believers. That is why He designed a way for His Spirit to dwell in us, so that we might commune with Him forever.

When God saves us, He calls us into a personal relationship with the Holy Spirit. He gives us new life, and we become spiritually alive, and begin a new life under a new master, our Lord Jesus Christ. If we allow the Holy Spirit to lead us, He will help us discern between what is true and what is not, what is wise and what is foolish, etc. Each day, we must make many life decisions. Most of our decisions concern issues not clearly spelled out in the scriptures. As we are barraged with details of everyday living, the Holy Spirit will guide us and empower us to make the right choices.

Another important reason to be filled with the Spirit is that we exemplify God here on Earth. The Holy Spirit will empower us to achieve all things that God has predestined to take place in our lives. Without being filled with the Holy Spirit, we are powerless. It takes the indwelling of the Spirit for us to be bold in the Lord and to be witnesses who produce fruit. In John 14:12-13, Jesus proclaimed the following: "He that believes in Me and the works that I do he shall do also; and greater works than these shall he do because I go unto my Father—And whatever you ask in my name, that will I do, that my Father may be glorified in the Son." When we became Christians, we were relegated the power to use the name of the Lord Jesus—but not until we receive the Baptism of the Holy Spirit are we able to use the power from God—that power makes our lives unsinkable.

Chapter 25

Worldly Conditions

The conditions in the world during Jesus' time were much like the world is today. In the first century, Europe, England, Egypt, Asia Minor, and the whole Middle East were a part of Rome's empire. The country spoke many languages, people were constantly adapting to the customs of conquering nations, and slavery was the accepted practice. Women were treated as lower class. They were denied educational opportunities. As babies they were exposed to the elements and left to die as boys were preferred. Under the iron heal of Rome, everything was heavily taxed. This practice equated to taxation without representation. The rich got richer, and the poor got poorer. This practice continues today.

During the first century, several religious sects surfaced, three of which the Pharisees, the Sadducees, and the Sanhedrin (a supreme religious body with no power). The Pharisees were a small group of influential men who claimed to follow every detail of God's Law. They believed that both the

Scripture and the Rabbi's interpretations of Scripture were equally binding. Jesus followed the Scripture but ignored the interpretation of the Rabbi's. The Pharisees quickly became Jesus' enemies.

The Sadducees were wealthy men who controlled the priesthood. They were rivals of the Pharisees and recognized only the first five books of the Old Testament as Scripture. They were materialistic in their thinking and even denied the resurrection of Jesus. The Sadducees retained older interpretation of the Mosaic Law against the oral tradition. They added whatever they wanted to say. They joined the Pharisees in opposing Jesus, who they saw as a threat to their wealth and power. Even though Jesus preached and taught and performed miracles to support His Godly message, these religious leaders openly attacked Jesus, and tried to undermine Him in any way they could. They used their powers of excommunication to punish those who supported Jesus. Some religious sects continue this practice of excommunication today, even if certain interpretations of man are not followed.

In Romans 1: 21-32, the Apostle Paul clearly portrays the inevitable downward spiral into sin. First, people reject God; next, they make up their own ideas of what God should be and do; then they fall into sin. This includes sexual sin, greed, hatred, envy, murder, fighting, lying, bitterness, and gossip. Finally, they grow to hate God and encourage others to do so, too. God does not cause this steady progression toward evil. Rather, when people reject Him, He allows them to live as they choose. God gives them over to their sinful desires. In Leviticus 18:22, homosexuality is strictly forbidden. Yet, this sin has been commonly practiced since the creation of man. Even today, homosexuality is widely practiced; same-sex marriage has been legalized. It is evident that when we abandon God and suppress the truth about Him, we open ourselves up to all that is evil. The very existence of such evils in society is evidence of man's abandonment of God, for where God is known and loved, such behavior is unthinkable.

About the Authors

VINCENT BROWN

Vincent Brown (1937-2020) was a native of Washington, D.C. After a brief stint in the U. S. Air Force, he began his career in the Federal Government. He spent most of his career at the Department of Health and Human Services, Food and Drug Administration. While employed, he completed ad hoc courses at Cornell and the University of Maryland. In 1996, he retired with 41 years of federal service. While he had an illustrious career, he had the burning desire to learn more about the Holy Scriptures. Subsequently, he graduated, with honors, from The Jericho Christian Training College. He was the Lay Minister for Discipleship at the Church of St. Martin de Porres. When time permitted, he loved to write. He was a prolific writer, hence "The Blessed Man."

MAXINE BROWN

Maxine grew up in Southeastern Virginia. Her educational aspirations brought her to the Washington, D.C. Metropolitan Area. This is a snapshot of her career path. Environmental Science Services Administration—she was on the Editorial Staff at the National Earthquake Information Center; Bureau of the

Census—she assisted in developing videotapes for former Census Bureau Director, Jack Keane, and she wrote the script for a training videotape featuring Henry Cisneros, former Mayor of San Antonio. She was Special Assistant to the Associate Director for Statistical Design, Methodology, and Standards. In response to the Clinton-Gore mandate for federal agencies to conduct customer satisfaction surveys, she was detailed to the University of Maryland, Joint Program for Survey Methodology, to assist in designing training courses for the federal government. Maxine wore a genuine NASA space suit, badge, and cap to present an overview of the Census Bureau's newly designed travel management system and she and her staff received permission from NASA to dub the actual lift-off and landing of a space shuttle. She retired from the Census Bureau as Assistant Division Chief of Administrative and Customer Services.

Maxine currently resides in Maryland; her passion is gardening.

In Memory of

Vincent Harold Brown, Sr.

(November 14, 1937~February 23, 2020)

Planted a Betty Magnolia tree in his memory in July 2020.

Dedicated the tree on September 11, 2021.

Installed a memorial plaque at the base of the tree.

Released 50 Monarch butterflies to the tune of *Wings of a Butterfly* by Jimmie Scott and sung by Shauna Chanda.

Made in United States
North Haven, CT
20 July 2022